Centerville Library
Washington-Centerville Public Library
Centerville, Ohio

CALIFORNIA FIGHTS BACK

D1399626

Also by Peter Schrag

Paradise Lost:
California's Experience, America's Future (1998)

California: America's High-Stakes Experiment (2006)

Not Fit for Our Society:
Immigration and Nativism in America (2010)

When Europe Was a Prison Camp: Father and Son
Memoirs, 1940–1941 (with Otto Schrag) (2015)

CALIFORNIA FIGHTS BACK

The Golden State in the Age of Trump

Peter Schrag

Heyday, Berkeley, California

Copyright © 2018 by Peter Schrag

All rights reserved.
Published in the United States by Heyday. No portion of this work may be reproduced or transmitted in any form or by any means, electronic or mechanical, including photocopying and recording, or by any information storage or retrieval system, without permission in writing from Heyday.

Book and cover design by Ashley Ingram

Library of Congress Cataloging-in-Publication Data

Names: Schrag, Peter, author.
Title: California fights back : the Golden State in the age of Trump / Peter
  Schrag.
Description: Berkeley, California : Heyday, 2018.
Identifiers: LCCN 2017051359 | ISBN 9781597144476 (pbk. : alk. paper)
Subjects: LCSH: Political planning--California. | Political
  culture--California. | Liberalism--California. | California--Politics and
  government--21st century. | United States--Politics and government--2017-
Classification: LCC JK8749.P64 S44 2018 | DDC 320.9794--dc23
LC record available at https://lccn.loc.gov/2017051359

E-book ISBN: 978-1-59714-449-0

Printed in East Peoria, Illinois by Versa Press, Inc.

10 9 8 7 6 5 4 3 2 1

Europeans have long marveled at the driving force, the "restless energy," of America; but it is only in California that this energy is coeval with statehood.... In California the lights went on all at once, in a blaze, and they have never dimmed.

—Carey McWilliams,
California: The Great Exception (1949)

Prologue

California's battle against the Washington of Donald Trump, Paul Ryan, Mitch McConnell—and the increasingly influential fringe represented by Steve Bannon and Alabama's Roy Moore—encompasses two strands tightly woven around each other. One is the determined fight, wherever possible, against the cruelty and inanity of an administration and congressional majority hell-bent on rolling back the programs and policies of enlightened self-interest enacted over the better part of a century under both Republican and Democratic administrations. The other is a defense of California's progressive, if still imperfect, success as a model for the nation and the world. The first would not be possible without the second and is inextricably tied to it.

But this is not just the story of a left coast state resisting a revanchist ultraconservative national government that seems to have gone off the rails, the un-Texas of 2018. It's also a story about the confrontation of reason against unreason, of a belief in knowledge against denial, distortion, lies, and a prideful lack of curiosity.

And because a similar strain of racism, unreason, and denial embedded itself in the Republican Party well before Trump became a candidate, it will probably outlast him. "Donald Trump is not an outlier," Barack Obama told the *New Yorker*'s David Remnick shortly after the 2016 election. "He is a culmination, a logical conclusion of the rhetoric and tactics of the Republican Party for the past ten, fifteen, twenty years. What surprised me was the degree to which those tactics and rhetoric completely jumped the rails. There were no governing principles, there was no one to say, 'No, this is going too far, this isn't what we stand for.'"

In the GOP, the first of Trump's qualifications for high office was his baseless racist "Birther" charge, contra all evidence, that Obama was not born in the United States, followed by his attacks on Mexicans as "bad hombres," his vow to stop all Muslims from entering the United States because they might be terrorists, his fiction about widespread voter fraud, all laced with his indifference to the truth about almost everything. What's highly probable is that without determined, reasoned resistance, the divisiveness and distrust that Trump fanned and exploited—and the accompanying erosion of American democracy—may poison the nation's politics and public policy long after he's gone from office.

And Trump could be gone sooner than anyone expected when he was elected. After his failure to condemn the neo-Nazi thugs in Charlottesville—the praise with faint damns—and the resulting exodus of corporate executives who should have been his closest allies from his advisory councils; his personal attacks on congressional leaders of his own party; his bratty threat, quickly withdrawn, to shut down the government if Congress did not approve his wall at the border; his string of impetuous flips, and the ongoing investigations into the Trump family's connections with the Russians, Trump's early departure seemed possible even before the 2018 midterm elections.

Even for Trump haters talking impeachment, that could be a mixed blessing. Trump's megalomania, racism, misogyny, polarizing personality, his conflicts of interest, his juvenile bullying and daily tantrums have served to impede, if not stop, a broad right-wing agenda that's nearly unprecedented in American politics. At the same time Trump's behavior has been an incomparable motivator and fundraiser for liberal groups, from the ACLU and Common Cause to Planned Parenthood, the Environmental Defense Fund, the League of Conservation Voters, and the various wings of the Democratic Party. Without those distractions, this Congress and a White House occupied by Mike Pence, surely the most determined and doctrinaire conservative to hold that office since World War II, and a close ally of the Koch brothers, may be more focused, unified, and politically effective than they could ever be with a crazy uncle raging in the party's attic.

Republicans celebrate Ronald Reagan as one of their heroes, but it's unlikely that they would now recognize him as one of their own, a sunny pragmatist who signed hefty tax increases both as California's governor and as president, signed California's Therapeutic Abortion Act, supported an ambitious California program of parkland acquisition, and as president negotiated a major nuclear force reduction treaty with the Russians. In the 1980s, he seemed to a lot of his opponents like an extreme conservative. Today he would be regarded as a moderate. Trump has been a dream for energizing moderates and liberals but his departure, whenever it comes, will leave much of the anger, distrust, and divisiveness he fueled festering behind. Without him, a Pence administration and this Republican Congress, while less likely to blunder into nuclear war, could be even more difficult to resist.

But that quandary makes resistance to the powers in Washington even more critical. And there is no state, no party, no institution, no organization better positioned to mount that resistance than California, the nation's largest state, the world's sixth-largest economy, an ethnically diverse majority-minority state that has thrived in large part through the immigration that produced that diversity. California is the nation's leader, and often the world's, in progressive energy policy and in reducing its per capita consumption of water, fossil fuels, and other natural resources; in creating the technologies of the future; in celebrating the rich cultural mix, in music and art, in food, in language and cultural traditions that its diversity produces. It is, as the following pages should make clear, the nearest thing to a hopeful model for the nation's future and the most powerful and persuasive alternative to the course that the wreckers in Washington are so relentlessly pursuing.

PETER SCHRAG
Oakland
November 2017

California Fights Back

I

IT'S BEEN JUST A HALF CENTURY SINCE THE writer Joan Didion, a native daughter, reminded us that the stakes for democracy might be higher in California than anywhere else in America. This is the place, she wrote, "in which the mind is troubled by some buried but ineradicable suspicion that things had better work here, because here, beneath that immense bleached sky, is where we run out of continent."

Things have not always worked well in the Golden State. Californians cheered in the months after Pearl Harbor when 120,000 ethnic Japanese, many U.S. citizens among them, were driven from their homes and land and imprisoned in distant internment camps. Californians demanded the exclusion of Chinese immigrants in the last quarter of the nineteenth century and of Mexicans in the twentieth; they herded the Okies fleeing the dust bowl into miserable camps; in the decades after the Gold Rush, they murdered Indians by the thousands. In the fifties, Hollywood blacklisted liberal writers and directors; the University of California required all faculty to take a loyalty oath, while the state senate's Tenney Committee was relentless in its pursuit of alleged communists. More immediately, as this story should make clear, the California of the 1980s and 1990s looked like much of the America of 2018: fearful, xenophobic, distrustful of government and its own institutions, a state in revolt, it seemed, against its own welcoming, tolerant recent past.

But in the past decade, it's recovered, indeed dramatically reversed itself—on immigrants and race, on trust in government, on taxation and public goods, on crime and human freedom. It's regained some of its optimism. It still has a plethora of serious problems and its strain of ethnic prejudice and nativism may never be fully eradicated. But both the history of California's recovery and the story of what it's become since are the nearest we have to a model alternative to where Washington's leaders now want to take the nation.

So, California's resistance to Trump is not merely a defense of its programs and policies on health, the environment, immigration, and in the treatment of minorities—itself a word with very different meanings in a place where all ethnic groups are minorities and an increasing percentage of residents are of mixed or altogether undetermined ethnicities. It is also a defense, or maybe a celebration, of the California alternative. After Charlottesville and Trump's failure to loudly condemn the gun-toting Nazis and racists responsible for the violence there, after his relentless attack on Muslims and his campaigns against immigrants and so much else, California's pluralism—of race, religion, ethnicity, gender, and cultures—and the resulting economic success is itself a model for the nation and a damning indictment of those who pretend to lead it. Needless to say, the stakes couldn't be greater, both for the state and for the United States. Anyone who thinks about this country must know it.

GIVEN CALIFORNIA'S SIZE, demographic diversity, economic heft, and its (mostly) blue political hue, it's not surprising that the state is both the leader of the resistance to the reactionary drift, and often the mindlessness, in Washington and, at the same time, a bright model of an alternative. And while there was never a chance that it would—or could—secede from the union, as some proposed (and some still do), California, which has always had some centrifugal impulses, behaves increasingly like an independent nation.

None of it was inevitable. Forty years ago, in June 1978, in a major shift from the ebullient, progressive decades that followed World War II, California voters, by a margin of nearly two to one, passed Proposition 13, which slashed local property taxes by nearly 60 percent, sharply constraining all public services, and made California the epicenter of the national tax revolt, what Robert Kuttner called "the revolt of the haves." It also sparked a wave of voter initiatives, most of them, though not all, conservative—on crime, taxation and state spending, gay marriage, education, the environment, water—that tied government into knots and obviated any populist Tea Party uprising in California. Proposition 13 and its progeny, screaming expressions of distrust in the normal governmental process, was California's rolling Tea Party revolt. In parts of the California interior, many of which voted for Trump, that's still the predominant mood.

But probably the most critical political event of that era was the passage in 1994, with the strong backing of Republican Governor Pete Wilson, of Proposition 187 ("Save Our State"), an anti-immigrant ballot measure that would have equaled anything that Donald Trump has yet proposed. On the same day, the voters also passed "three strikes," the most severe criminal sentencing law in the nation, a law that even a hard-liner like Attorney General Jeff Sessions might now dream about.

Proposition 187 would have denied all public services, including schooling and all but emergency health care, to all undocumented immigrants. It would have required public employees —teachers, police officers, doctors, and social workers—to report every undocumented immigrant they came across to the state's attorney general and/or federal immigration officials. It was soon blocked as unconstitutional by a federal judge, but not before the resulting panic drove thousands of undocumented immigrants underground, and before Wilson, running a blatantly anti-immigrant TV campaign, parlayed it into his come-from-behind reelection victory. (After the failure of Congress to act on comprehensive immigration reform, it also became a spur to local and state action elsewhere.) In 1996, California voters, again with strong support from Wilson, passed Proposition 209, which banned affirmative action by race or gender in public education, public employment, and contracting. In 1998, they piled it on with Proposition 227, funded by a Silicon Valley millionaire named Ron Unz, which denied bilingual education to any student whose parents did not demand it.

Now California, with some 39 million people, is an ethnically majority-minority state and will soon have an absolute Latino majority. Roughly 2.5 million (in 2014) of the state's residents are undocumented, a number that may be going down as Mexico's birthrate declines and its economy improves and as Trump's government becomes more hostile. The majority of those undocumented immigrants are from Latin America, but others come from almost every country on earth. And contra the general belief, no doubt including Trump's, that they all slipped over the Mexican border, nationwide about 40 percent are visa overstayers, according to the Pew Research Center and the U.S. Department of Homeland Security, and far and away the largest number of them are from Canada. They're visitors who entered legally and just never left. Where in 1994 California passed Proposition 187 and ordered cops and other public employees to report undocumented immigrants to federal authorities, it's now passing sanctuary bills to prohibit them from doing precisely that.

At last count, the state's economy was the sixth-largest on earth, just behind the United Kingdom, and just ahead of France. California is the nation's largest center of trade with Asia, Latin America, and Canada, and despite dire warnings from conservatives about the dangers of "job-killing" tax increases, it's enacted three major tax increases in the past decade and regained a larger percentage of jobs lost in the 2008 recession than the nation as a whole—far more than famously low-tax states whose governors and business leaders, among them former Texas governor Rick Perry, were always said to be in California luring away its employers. In 2016, California's GDP grew at nearly twice the rate of the national economy. Between 2012 and 2016, California accounted for 17 percent of U.S. job growth, even as air quality in the Bay Area and Southern California improved. Thus, said Steve Levy of the Center for the Continuing Study of the California Economy, Trump's claim that regulations and the Paris climate agreement are job killers "is just wrong."

While Trump is trying to boost the coal and oil industry and reopening federal lands to mining and other commercial exploitation, California, which aims to rely on an average of 50 percent non-fossil fuels in its energy mix by 2030, has become by far the nation's leader in reducing its reliance on fossil fuels and, through higher efficiency standards for everything from light bulbs and refrigerators to home insulation, consumes less energy per resident than any other state. In the spring of 2017, it set records for the percentage of renewables—wind and solar—providing power to the state's electricity grid, on one day briefly reaching 67 percent of the mix, not counting hydro, according to the Independent System Operator, which controls 80 percent of the grid.

And while the White House and Congress were mired in chaos, California passed a massive long-term infrastructure bill—roads, bridges, transit, water systems—to the tune of $5 billion a year in additional gas and other vehicle taxes: precisely what Trump promised the nation in his campaign and which he still isn't close to delivering. In Hollywood and Silicon Valley, and in the influential devices, systems, and designs— in clothes, cars, phones, games, on the web— often emanating from the melding of the two,

California is probably the nation's most powerful cultural influence, and perhaps the world's, and a driver of technological change as rapid and profound—and for many not educated or trained for it, no doubt, as unsettling—as any in history.

California's majority Democrats labeled the state spending plan enacted in June 2017, with its $45 million in taxpayer funding for the legal representation of undocumented immigrants facing deportation, their "protect and persist" budget. "While the $183.2-billion spending outline only rarely veers into direct confrontations with federal policy," in the words of John Myers of the *Los Angeles Times*, probably the most insightful California political reporter today, "legislative leaders nonetheless see it as a national example—an alternative view on the role of government." Indeed, the entire 2017 legislative session, from January to September, was laced with anti-Trump bills, budget items, resolutions, and rhetoric, among them an education grant program linking the wartime internment of Japanese Americans to Trump's travel ban on "immigrants and refugees from Muslim-majority countries." California, the Democratic leaders in the legislature declared within a day of Trump's election, would now be "the keeper of the nation's future." In the view of optimists like the late California historian Kevin Starr, of course, it always had been.

Two decades after the state voted for Proposition 187, 85 percent of Californians, including 65 percent of California Republicans, now tell the pollsters that if undocumented immigrants meet certain conditions they should be allowed to stay legally and become citizens. In 2016, Hillary Clinton, carrying even such long-time GOP strongholds as Orange County, beat Trump in California by more than four million votes, with a margin of 61–39, greater than any other state's. Without them, she would have lost the nationwide popular vote. California, in effect, voted one way while the rest of the nation voted another way. On the same day, with Proposition 58, the voters repealed the barriers to bilingual education they'd voted for in 1998.

Because of the state's diversity and mixed economy, most Californians now understand intuitively that their southern border, with its thousands of binational institutions and activities—in commerce, in water management and energy resources, in health, in environmental policy, in education, and with its tens of thousands of cross border families—is no longer a line that can be marked by a "wall," but a region. Every day in this bilingual, bicultural region, uncounted thousands cross the border to attend American schools. Hundreds of thousands cross to work, shop, get medical care, for entertainment, or to visit. Goods worth tens of millions cross daily in both directions. Talk about building a "wall" along that border is a bit like King Canute trying to stop the waves. In a survey conducted in 2017, the Public Policy Institute of California (PPIC), found that "solid majorities" of all California ethnic groups (82 percent of Latinos and African Americans; 60 percent of non-Hispanic whites; 72 percent of Asians) oppose Trump's wall.

Governor Pete Wilson was reelected in the anti-immigrant wave of 1994. But with the exception of the election of Arnold Schwarzenegger in the bizarre recall in 2003 of Governor Gray Davis, a man who was deeply disliked even in his own party and politically battered by the industry-manipulated electricity crisis of 2000–2001, California has elected no Republican to a major state office since Schwarzenegger's reelection in 2006. In 2017, both houses of the legislature had two-to-one Democratic supermajorities. All the constitutional officers, from governor and attorney general to insurance commissioner and state school superintendent, are Democrats. Both U.S. senators are Democrats.

And while both parties have declined in registration, the Republicans, thanks to Wilson's immigrant bashing, and to the party's decades-long inhospitality to women and ethnic minorities, have lost far more voters to other parties, or to "decline to state," than the Democrats. In 1992, 39 percent of the state's voters called themselves Republicans. By 2016, that number had declined to 26 percent. California's delegation in the House is now composed of thirty-nine Democrats and fourteen Republicans. Of those Republicans, all of whom voted to repeal the Affordable Care Act in 2017, as many as six or seven could lose their seats in 2018. And that Democratic edge comes without partisan gerrymandering. In California, a nonpartisan reapportionment commission now draws both legislative and congressional districts.

II

THE PARADIGMATIC TURNAROUND MOMENT, ironically, came in 2005 under the Republican who sometimes called himself "the governator." There was no way to predict at the time that a dozen years later Arnold Schwarzenegger would taunt Trump as sharply as he taunted Democrats in his first years as California's governor. But his political conversion came long before, and represents a little-recognized watershed event.

With one major exception—that unlike Trump, Schwarzenegger (almost literally) had made himself, without help from his father's millions—Schwarzenegger in many ways was very much like Trump. A bodybuilder and movie actor, he was a narcissistic show business celebrity who had never held public office before; a misogynist with a trail of sexual harassment and groping accusations behind him (he later grudgingly apologized for his behavior on those "rowdy movie sets"); and a man who, in that pretweet era, had a mouth sometimes as much out of control as Trump's would be a dozen years later: In his first years in Sacramento, he called the Democrats "girlie men." He referred to the state attorney general, the treasurer, and state superintendent of schools, all Democrats who opposed his measures, as the "Three Stooges." He labeled public-sector workers, members of powerful unions—nurses, cops, firefighters, teachers—"special interests." He echoed Grover Norquist, the nation's most vociferous anti-taxer: "We don't want to feed the monster (of public spending)," he told the editorial board of the *Sacramento Bee.* "We want to feed the private sector and starve the public sector." He drove his gas-guzzling Hummer in defiance of all the environmentalists' calls for conservation. He loudly proclaimed his intention to "blow up the boxes" of the government bureaucracy and "clean house."

Unlike Trump, he began his first term with high public approval ratings, but in less than two years they sank from nearly 70 percent to 40 percent. And as things turned sour, he took a cue from his predecessor Pete Wilson's immigrant bashing just a decade before. He called for closing the border and endorsed the work of the minuteman group of vigilantes who were patrolling it.

The crunch came in a special election that Schwarzenegger, in support of five ballot measures he was backing, had called in November 2005, when the state's voters, irritated in part that they had to vote in a state election for the fourth time in four years, trashed all five. One would have severely curtailed the political clout of public-sector unions by requiring them to get annual consent from each member before his or her dues could be used for political activities. Those members, having been attacked as special interests, hounded him so incessantly during the campaign that he had to slip into his own events through the back doors of the hotels they were held in. They also appeared in union-funded TV ads—a nurse, a firefighter, a teacher, as nice, friendly, public servants, not "special interests." Another Schwarzenegger-backed initiative would have radically changed the compensation and tenure laws for public school teachers; a third sought to amend the constitution to further restrain state spending, already severely limited by prior ballot measures; and yet another required physicians to inform parents before performing an abortion on a minor. When one movie bombs, he said as his losses piled up on election night, there's always another.

And indeed, there was. Even before the votes were counted, the governor, aware of the public mood, the state's changing ethnic and generational demographics, the rapidly growing support in California for undocumented immigrants, and his own decline in the polls, began to change his tune. Where everything had once been negative, there was now a positive agenda, a new tone, and a new staff, among them, as Schwarzenegger's chief of staff, Susan Kennedy, a married, cigar-smoking lesbian, who had been chief of staff for Governor Gray Davis, the Democrat whom Schwarzenegger replaced in the recall election in 2003.

The new program, launched in Schwarzenegger's 2006 reelection campaign, was nothing if not ambitious: substantially reduce California's greenhouse gas emissions and cut global warming; provide every Californian with health care; use the state's stem cell research program to find treatments for Alzheimer's and Parkinson's; and build, build, build—roads, schools, flood control structures.

The refrain now was cooperation—not bipartisanship, he said, but "post-partisanship." And the rhetoric, if not the vision, was nothing if not grand. He would show a politically gridlocked national government how to get things done; he would carry the message about global warming to the world. In the summer of 2006, as he was running for reelection, he signed an "agreement" with British Prime Minister Tony Blair on developing coordinated policies on climate control. In the same year, the Democratic legislature passed, and the Republican governor signed, an increase in the state's minimum wage and approved $37 billion in bonds, the largest bond package to date, for road construction, schools, and flood control. The showman-politician, who'd taken a dive in the polls two years before, won reelection by a handy margin in 2006 and now had the approval of 60 percent of the voters. If he had been born in the United States, he would automatically have been high on the list of possible presidential candidates.

"I believe," he said in his 2007 state of the state address, "that together we can not only lead California into the future...we can show the nation and the world how to get there. We can do this because we have the economic strength; we have the population and the technological force of a nation-state. We are the modern equivalent of the ancient city-states of Athens and Sparta. California has the idea of Athens and the power of Sparta." His proposal to provide health care to every one of California's 6.5 million uninsured residents was always unrealistic, but it clearly signaled, three years before Obamacare was enacted, that the country was ready for that "conversation." A Rip Van Winkle who'd fallen asleep in 2004 would have hardly recognized Schwarzenegger when he woke up in 2006.

It wasn't poetry and a great many of the old problems remained unsolved, but it was certainly grandiose. It was the same old Schwarzenegger, but with a very different program. It would also turn out to be an outline of what California would be doing a decade later. Schwarzenegger seemed to recognize that in its pluralism, in its high-tech economy, in its regional multiethnic culture—in music, in art and literature, in food (kosher burritos? kosher Thai fish sauce? Szechuan guacamole?), in the growing rate of intermarriage, and in its millions of mixed, cross border families and relationships—and in so much else, California was the most hopeful possible model for the nation's future. If you looked at the faces in any graduating class at the University of California at Berkeley, the most highly regarded of the nation's public universities, you'd be hard-pressed to tell who was Indian or Pakistani, who was Mexican, who was Brazilian, who was Iranian, who was Korean or Chinese, and who was (by whatever definition) "American." As Schwarzenegger's second term began, a lot of Republicans regarded him as a turncoat, a RINO, Republican in name only; conversely, it was hard to find a Democrat who now spoke ill of him. In 2007, ten months after his reelection, Schwarzenegger warned his fellow Republicans they were "not filling the seats" and "dying at the box office" because they wouldn't recognize their state's emerging pluralism.

Jerry Brown's campaign for governor in 2010 tried hard to make his opponent, Meg Whitman, sound like an echo of the first Schwarzenegger. But when Brown, who had been governor 1975–83, succeeded Schwarzenegger in 2011 (which happened to be near the beginning of the national economic recovery following the implosion of 2008), it seemed less a change than a continuation.

Gray Davis, the governor who was famously recalled in 2003, only the second governor in American history to suffer that fate (and once chief of staff in the first Jerry Brown administration), wisely observed that when things go well, the governor gets more credit than he's earned; when they go badly, he gets more blame than he deserves. And that's no doubt true for Brown, who, taking office in 2011, would preside in good economic times—in California, because of its steeply graduated (and dangerously volatile) income tax, when the rich get richer, the state gets richer even faster, and when the economy goes down, the state loses more. But Brown, with his famously parsimonious streak, also restrained the big spenders among his fellow Democrats in the legislature, so that the chronic deficits of the decades after the passage of Proposition 13 became modest budget surpluses—at least when the state's unfunded pension liabilities weren't counted—and more money went to reserves. That, in turn, helped earn him the voter confidence to pass his big tax increases, again on high incomes and in the sales tax, not on middle incomes.

AFTER DONALD TRUMP WAS ELECTED IN 2016, there was a flurry of talk in California about secession, sometimes called Calexit, which a quirky political activist named Louis Marinelli launched before Trump's election, though it got little attention until after. During his political career, Marinelli had shuttled from working for the maverick centrist John Edwards to the sponsorship of initiatives to stop same-sex marriage. He now lives in Yekaterinburg, Russia, where he teaches English.

Secession was always a quixotic idea, an impossibility given the insurmountable political, constitutional, and economic hurdles confronting it. Nonetheless, Marinelli's Calexit campaign generated some respectful attention from the American media, as weird California things often do, and got a good deal of agitprop attention and support from the Russians—as with Brexit, for the Kremlin this might have seemed another chance to stir up a little disunion in the West. Marinelli even claimed to have opened a California "embassy" in Moscow. But he soon faced the inevitable, gave up the California secession campaign, and applied for Russian citizenship.

The demise of Calexit didn't end it. In July, a group calling itself the California Freedom Coalition began to circulate petitions to qualify a ballot measure that would direct the governor and California's congressional representatives to "negotiate continually greater autonomy from [the] federal government, up to and including agreement establishing California as a fully independent country."

That improbable proposal was not likely to have any more success than Calexit. But once Donald Trump won in the Electoral College and became president, California began to pursue a course of resistance that in another era could have been arguably described as interposition or nullification—not secession but halfway to it. And given Trump's rhetoric, it's hard to say that it was unprovoked. "If we have to, we'll defund (California)," Trump, barely two weeks in office, said early in February 2017 in an interview with his friend Bill O'Reilly, at the time still with Fox. "We give tremendous amounts of money to California. California in many ways is out of control." (And, contra Trump's claim, as many California secessionists have pointed out, Californians pay more in federal taxes than the state gets back in federal funding. Democrats in blue California subsidize the Republicans in the low-tax red states.)

Even before Trump was elected, California's overwhelmingly Democratic legislature passed the "Trust Act" of 2013, which prohibits county jail officials from holding undocumented inmates who have not been convicted of serious felonies for ICE (Immigration and Customs Enforcement) and deportation when their jail terms end. Continue with AB 493, passed in August 2017, which prohibits law enforcement officers from detaining any crime victim or witness on an immigration violation, except under court order, and AB 21, passed the following month, which urges the University of California, and requires the state's other public colleges, to "adopt and implement a policy limiting assistance with immigration enforcement to the fullest extent possible consistent with federal and state law including providing guidance to all faculty, staff and students informing them of their rights under state or federal law and how to respond to federal immigration action or order."

Now add SB 54, the "California Values Act," which prohibits state and local law enforcement officers from detaining, arresting, or interrogating undocumented immigrants for "immigration enforcement purposes." It would also "limit assistance with immigration enforcement to the fullest extent possible consistent with federal and state law at public schools, public libraries, health facilities operated by the state or...courthouses."

The act, passed in the last hours of the 2017 legislative session, had been considerably revised to accommodate objections from Governor

Jerry Brown and from police and sheriffs' organizations who warned that the bill would make Californians less safe. (More persuasively, its backers contend it will make Californians safer by encouraging cooperation between immigrant communities and the cops.) And so its protections don't apply to violent felons, repeat offenders, and those jailed for some eight hundred "wobblers"—crimes that could be charged as either felonies or misdemeanors. It's not the "sanctuary law" as some headlines had it. It may not be more than a declaration of good intentions, "a measure," as senate president pro tem Kevin de Léon, its sponsor, said, "that reflects the values of who we are as a great state." But good intentions in the current political environment are still worth a lot.

Sessions called the act "unconscionable." Brown, in reply, called it "a reaction to the kind of xenophobia we see coming out of Washington." The bill, Brown said in a signing statement, itself unusual, "strikes a balance that will protect safety, while bringing a measure of comfort to those families who are now living in fear every day." But Brown, in adding a paragraph on what it "does not do"—doesn't prevent federal immigration enforcement agents "from doing their work in any way"—made the signing statement almost seem like the groundwork for any legal defense the state might need against a federal suit. As soon as Brown signed it, Tom Homan, ICE's acting director, said it would make ICE's job harder and threatened more arrests in the community—meaning more sweeps. Which, of course, ICE had already been engaged in.

California is already dotted with sanctuary cities—Berkeley, Fresno, Long Beach, Los Angeles, Oakland, Palm Springs, Richmond, San Bernardino, San Diego, San Francisco, San Jose, Santa Ana, among others—as well as the majority of the state's fifty-eight counties, most of which made the decision before Trump's election, that will not allow their resources to be used to detain undocumented immigrants for federal immigration officials. The Obama administration, hoping to sell comprehensive immigration reform to Congress by proving that it was in control of the border, broke prior records in the number of people it deported. But it appeared ambivalent on the sanctuary movement, condemning it but imposing sanctions that were relatively mild and in one case not imposed until Obama's last year in office. But noncooperation on anything affecting deportation seemed to drive Trump and Sessions crazy.

Two Bay Area counties, San Francisco and Santa Clara, successfully sued in federal court to block Trump's executive order, issued five days after his inauguration, seeking to take federal funding away from sanctuary cities. "The Constitution," said San Francisco's challenge to the order, citing the Tenth Amendment, "establishes a balance of power between the state and Federal governments, as well as among the coordinate branches of Federal government, to prevent the excessive accumulation of power in any single entity and reduce the risk of tyranny and abuse from any government office." The executive order, said the Santa Clara County complaint, "commandeers state and local officials, transforming them into federal apparatchiks and severing the bonds of political accountability inherent in our federal system." Apparatchiks.

But that was only the first skirmish in what would be a multiplicity of long legal battles on issues from immigration to offshore drilling to birth control under the Affordable Care Act. How will the courts finally rule when Washington begins cutting funding to sanctuary cities, or maybe states like California, and what funding can they cut? Jerry Brown, who still needed favorable decisions from Washington on federal funding for a number of costly California projects, among them electrification of a commuter rail line from San Francisco to Silicon Valley, and for his economically improbable high-speed rail service from San Francisco to Los Angeles, never publicly defined his reservations to the original version of SB 54. But, ever the Jesuit seminarian, he did say (on the NBC program "Meet the Press") that SB 54 is not a "sanctuary bill"—sanctuary, going back to the Middle Ages, he pointed out, was related to churches. Its goal, Brown said, "is to block and not to collaborate with abuse of federal power. That's the goal."

Still, there doesn't seem to be much doubt

that, as a consultant in the California legislature summarized it in her analysis of SB 54 and of Trump's threat to strip all sanctuary cities of their federal funding, that

> the federal government cannot force states to further its priorities in place of the state's. In fact, case law makes it clear that the federal government cannot do either of the following: 1) "commandeer" local officials by making them enforce federal laws (*Printz v. U.S.* (1997) 521 U.S. 898); or 2) force participation in a federal program by threatening to cut off federal funds, unless the funds are directly earmarked for that program.

Erwin Chemerinsky, dean of the UC Berkeley law school and a respected constitutional lawyer, agrees. "Under *Printz* and *NY v. US* (and for that matter *NFIB v. Sebelius*)," he wrote me in an email, "the threat to cut off funds to cities that do not cooperate with federal immigration officials violates the Tenth Amendment. The federal government cannot compel state and local action, or do it by putting strings on grants."

But how would the current Supreme Court, dominated by results-oriented conservatives—with perhaps one or two more to come—rule on sanctuary? In a number of recent high-profile cases—on voting rights, on campaign finance—it went out of its way to override precedent. In years past, the court consistently ruled, in cases striking down state laws to push out undocumented immigrants, "that the federal government [in the words of the National Immigration Law Center] has broad and exclusive power to regulate immigration." Could this court, especially after some future terrorist attack, use those same rulings to justify a crackdown on sanctuary? It's hard to imagine that Trump and Sessions won't try. At least one place, Miami-Dade County, fearing the loss of some federal funds, already seems to have capitulated, holding prisoners who are wanted for deportation after their jail terms ended. But Miami is not San Francisco or Los Angeles.

IV

CALIFORNIA HAS A WARM, SUNNY CLIMATE,
Jesse Unruh, the "Big Daddy" speaker of the
state assembly in the 1960s, was famously sup-
posed to have said, "which is why we have so
many fruits and nuts." But it may also be the
reason it's so hospitable to innovators; political, personal, and social experimentation; and
in-your-face independence. This is where people
came to remake themselves. California legalized
abortion seven years before *Roe v. Wade* (with a
bill Reagan signed) and passed the nation's first
medical marijuana law. California is the cradle
of American environmentalism, born in large
part from the very selfish motive of preserving the beauty of the place where Californians
live—nationalism of a very high order—and,
for nearly a half century, a major influence in

national policy. For Carey McWilliams, California, "the Great Exception," was "the edge of novelty."

Even in the first months of Trump's presidency, California's independent streak produced a long list of particulars. In that effort, probably the most active figure has been attorney general Xavier Becerra, who's given resistance to Washington a priority as high as normal state business, perhaps higher. Governor Jerry Brown's decision to name him attorney general to replace Kamala Harris in January 2017 after her election to the U.S. Senate could by itself be taken as an indicator of the state's intention to resist the new regime in Washington. The son of Mexican immigrants who grew up in a one-room house in Sacramento, Becerra went on to Stanford and Stanford Law School, and most recently served for twenty-four years in the House, where for a time he chaired the Congressional Hispanic Caucus. In his first eight months as attorney general, he did the following:

1. Filed a federal suit similar to the one filed a few months before by San Francisco and Santa Clara counties, challenging a new U.S. Justice Department requirement that in order to qualify for certain federal crime prevention funds cities and counties (meaning sanctuary cities) must give jailhouse access to immigration agents and provide forty-eight hours' notice before releasing any immigrant sought by the feds. Those conditions, the suit says, constitute an "unconstitutional attempt to force California law enforcement officials to engage in federal immigration enforcement, rather than allow them to use their discretion to determine how best to keep their communities safe."

2. Sent a letter to Interior Secretary Ryan Zinke warning him that he will "take any and all action necessary to protect" the six environmentally important California national monuments, of 129 nationwide, whose status—to retain, reduce, or eliminate—was the subject of an unprecedented Trump-ordered "review." Among them: the Berryessa Snow, Giant Sequoia, and Mojave Trails monuments. Presidents from Theodore Roosevelt to Barack Obama designated those national monuments, Becerra wrote, knowing that "exploitation of these lands for short-term profit or expediency would permanently scar these national treasures in a way [that could never be repaired]." No national monument has ever been eliminated (some have been reduced in acreage) nor, as Becerra reminded Zinke, does the act empower any president to do so. Three months later, Zinke withdrew the California monuments from his hit list. All or parts of ten others elsewhere remained on the block.

3. Vowed to battle any administration attempt to open a huge area on the Pacific Coast to offshore drilling for oil and gas, as a Trump executive order issued in April 2017 would permit. In response to that order, the governors of all three West Coast states jointly issued a statement recalling "the oil-soaked beaches and wildlife and the devastating economic impact [of oil spills] to local communities and the fishing industry," among them the devastating spill in 1969 that fouled fifty miles of beaches from Santa Barbara south. Until the *Exxon Valdez* ran up on the rocks on the Alaska coast in 1989, it was the worst oil spill in American history and a major impetus for the environmental movement that followed.

4. Sued to stop Trump's attempt to build a wall at the Mexican border, contending that it violated federal environmental laws and that the order to build it violated the Constitution's separation of powers by giving the president authority "to waive state and local laws."

5. Sued to stop Trump's rollback of the requirement that employers cover contraceptives as part of their employees' health insurance under the Affordable Care Act. The rollback, the suit charged, was, in effect, unconstitutional discrimination against women.

6. Sued, and got a lower court order, to stop the EPA's delay of the implementation of new rules to reduce methane leaks, said to be among the most powerful accelerators of climate change, from the 100,000-plus oil and gas wells on federal lands.

7. Announced that he'll resist, by all means at his disposal, any attempts by the feds, as U.S. Attorney General Jeff Sessions would dearly like to do, to crack down on California residents using or growing cannabis under the state's liberal marijuana laws. In 1996, California, after a campaign funded largely by the billionaire financier George Soros, became the first state—there are now twenty-nine, plus the District of Columbia—to legalize the medical use of marijuana and thus launched the swing in public support for legalizing the drug, which in turn may make it hard now for Sessions to pursue his goal.

In the same vein, it may not have been entirely coincidence that a few days after Sessions urged federal prosecutors to file the toughest charges possible against crime suspects, a strategy Becerra called "crazy" and "stupid," the California senate passed a major reduction in sentences for certain drug crimes.

But that's hardly all of it. Any list of what California officials have done in the first months after the election also has to include

1. The ruling in the spring of 2017 of the state Air Resources Board (ARB), long the nation's leader in curbing greenhouse gas pollution, further tightening emissions standards for cars and trucks. The ruling came even as EPA Administrator Scott Pruitt, who as Oklahoma's attorney general had long been cozy with the oil and gas industry, was attacking California for trying to impose its energy rules on the rest of the country. Although Pruitt later announced that the administration was backing away from its threat to revoke California's long-standing statutory authority to set auto emission regulations that are tighter than the national standards, the appointment in October of William Wehrum, a notorious hard-liner on the issue, as the director of EPA's air and radiation division, again raised that possibility. A little later the ARB's hard-nosed chair, Mary Nichols, told a *New York Times* reporter that come hell or high water she had no intention of backing off: "We're standing firm. We're prepared to sue. We're prepared to do what we need to do." We dare you.

2. The refusal of Secretary of State Alex Padilla, in concert with many of his peers in other states, to provide voter data to Trump's election fraud commission. To comply, he said, "would only serve to legitimize the false and already debunked claims of massive voter fraud made by the President, the Vice President, and Kobach [Kris Kobach, the secretary of state of Kansas, and the commission's vice-chair], who has a long history of sponsoring discriminatory, anti-immigrant policies including voter suppression and racial profiling laws." The commission, Padilla said in a press handout, "is a waste of taxpayer money and a distraction from the real threats to the integrity of our elections today: aging voting systems and documented Russian interference in our elections."

3. Decisions of the California-based Ninth Circuit Court of Appeals, widely regarded as the most liberal of the circuit courts, upholding the rulings of a federal judge in Seattle blocking Trump's first Muslim travel ban, and that of federal judge Derrick Watson in Hawaii striking down key parts of a subsequent, somewhat narrower, travel ban designed to avoid the legal problems of the first. Both, the suits challenging the ban charged, were thinly disguised acts of religious discrimination and violations of immigration laws forbidding discrimination based on national origin. Trump's subsequent ban on travel, issued in September 2017, which is not strictly limited to Muslim countries and was more carefully constructed, may be harder to overturn. But it will never be free of the whiff of religious and ethnic bigotry that tainted the originals and was also blocked by Judge Watson.

4. The initiative taken in the fall of 2016, before the election, by CalPERS, the state's huge $330 billion public employee pension fund, in the formation of a global alliance of large investors that would use its combined shareholder clout to press companies with the most carbon emissions to reduce those emissions. Formation of the alliance was prompted by a CalPERS study showing that eighty companies among the ten thousand in its portfolio caused roughly 50 percent of the carbon emissions. And when Trump withdrew from the Paris climate accords, the CalPERS board issued a statement saying, in effect, that Trump's decision was stupid. The Paris agreement, CalPERS said, "makes financial sense.... [It] enables us to manage material risk and build opportunity in our investment portfolio. Supporting its goals ultimately benefits our members and their long-term retirement security."

At the same time, Governor Jerry Brown was deeply involved with the United States Climate

Alliance, a group of fourteen states, all but two headed by Democrats, that were successfully reducing their share of the greenhouse gas emissions mandated by the Paris accords that Trump rejected.

In addition, there have been countless attempts, both by local public entities and private organizations, to fund the legal defense of undocumented immigrants—in cases like the Alum Rock School Board near San Jose, the defense of students—and challenge federal acts, and indeed, Trump's private interests. Among the most recent: a campaign by the liberal Courage Campaign to pressure CalPERS to divest from CIM Fund III, an investment group that pays the Trump organization millions to manage one of its luxury hotels. The wages of teachers, fighters, and other public employees, the Courage Campaign handout says, should not be invested in "Trump's shady, corrupt business empire." And in what may have been a little too much like preaching to the converted, the Courage Campaign briefly posted a huge sign on a billboard at the San Francisco–Oakland Bay

Bridge with a picture of a scowling Trump and the huge letters "IMPEACH."

And, as in many other states, California protestors, many with moving stories about chronically ill children or aging parents, jammed the town hall meetings of Republican members of the House, those with the courage to show up, who had voted to repeal the Affordable Care Act, and pelted them with questions. In Southern California, liberals organized "town halls" for Representatives Ed Royce, Duncan Hunter, and other Republican House members who didn't show up. At one, Democratic members of Congress, among them Representatives Linda Sanchez and Ted Lieu, then filled Royce's "empty chair" in what became a Democratic strategy meeting. The failure of the Senate to repeal the act may reduce a little of the heat under the Republicans but, given a host of other issues—and given the incessant Republican efforts to sabotage it—won't eliminate it.

Now add to the list the we-dare-you letter that lawyers for the leaders of the legislature, all Democrats, sent in April to Sessions and John

Kelly, now White House chief of staff, who was at that time the secretary of homeland security. The letter was itself a response to one Sessions and Kelly wrote in reaction to the demand from California Chief Justice Tani Cantil-Sakauye, a Sacramento-born Filipina who had been appointed by Schwarzenegger, that federal immigration agents stop "stalking courthouses and arresting undocumented immigrants." Such measures, she said, "not only compromise our core value of fairness, but they undermine the judiciary's ability to provide equal access to justice." Four months later, Cantil-Sakauye reiterated the complaint. ICE, she said, was continuing to do the same thing "in full force" in courthouses all over the country. "We are seeing people not come into court, not reporting to court, not reporting for services, not coming to testify."

The Sessions and Kelly letter charged that the state and "many of its largest cities and counties have enacted statutes and ordinances [to] hinder ICE from enforcing immigration law by prohibiting communication with ICE and denying requests by ICE officers and agents to enter prisons and jails to make arrests."

What specific laws, the legislators' letter asked, were Sessions and Kelly referring to? "The Administration appears to forget that our system [quoting a 1991 U.S. Supreme Court opinion] is one of 'dual sovereignty between the states and the Federal Government.'" The letter didn't deter the Justice Department from threatening a long list of sanctuary cities and states with the loss of federal law enforcement grants if they didn't agree to hold undocumented immigrant convicts for federal agents when their jail terms ended, but neither did the threat from the feds seem to have changed any minds in California's sanctuary cities, which claimed they were already in compliance with federal law.

John C. Calhoun of South Carolina, the great defender of the rights of the slave states, would have been familiar with the legislators' argument. A state, Calhoun had argued in his opposition to the federal Tariff Acts of 1828 and 1832, had the right to "interpose" itself to "arrest an unconstitutional act of the General

Government." A similar case was advanced by the abolitionist authors of the Massachusetts Personal Liberty Act of 1855, which made it an impeachable offense for state officials to help enforce the Fugitive Slave Act. But neither prevented the secession of the southern states or the Civil War that followed.

More recently, Alabama Governor George Wallace and Arkansas Governor Orval Faubus stood "in the schoolhouse door" to block court-ordered desegregation in southern classrooms.

And as any high school history student must know, state sovereignty and incipient rebellion are in our genetic makeup as a nation. That goes back at least to the Hartford Convention, where there was talk about the New England states negotiating a separate peace with England in the War of 1812, a threat serious enough for President Madison to move federal troops in case they were needed in Massachusetts or Connecticut—or indeed to the debates in the Constitutional Convention in 1787 itself, where the representatives of thirteen independent states met to form their "more perfect union" and where at least one, Rhode Island, wasn't sure it wanted to be part of that new nation at all. For nearly a decade, from 1836 to 1846, Texas was an independent nation. That history was invoked countless times in connection with the forty-five lawsuits that Texas officials filed challenging Obama administration programs. At one time, Texas Governor Rick Perry, later to become Trump's improbable secretary of energy, even uttered the word secession. Perry was author of a book published in 2010 entitled *Fed Up: Our Fight to Save America From Washington*, which could have become California's motto a few years later. Closer to home there was the (very) short-lived "California Republic," formed by a group of American rebels against the Mexican government in 1846, who seized military control of the Bay Area on the eve of the Mexican War. Its name is still on the state flag.

California would never follow Calhoun or the other secessionist precedents, nor could it. And no state measure, not the sanctuary laws nor the legal defense of immigrants that the state is helping fund, can stop the wave of ICE arrests and deportations that are generating fear among the undocumented and hundreds of thousands of their children and other family members, many of them citizens or legal residents. Moreover, the state will always be dependent on Washington, even the Washington of Trump and McConnell, for health care and education funding, for a large share of water management, for highway maintenance, and for emergency relief in the major disasters the state is prone to—fire, flood, the big earthquake that's high on the geologists' California calendar. While the terrible fires in October 2017 in Northern California were still raging, Brown asked Trump for federal aid—and quickly got it. In the end, we are still one nation.

Even declaring itself a "sanctuary state," as the papers originally described SB 54, may generate too much unnecessary internal friction with the conservative core of red counties in the state's interior and, worse, cloud its image of success and progressive programs east of the Sierra. To, in effect, officially throw itself in the way of federal law could make California look as extreme on the left as the self-destructive tax cuts in Kansas, or the campaign to destroy Planned Parenthood in Texas or Oklahoma, or the bills requiring transsexuals to use the bathrooms for the gender listed on their birth certificates, are on the right.

California has also given itself a black eye in the demand issued in the summer of 2017 by San Francisco's Democratic leaders that the National Park Service cancel the permit it had issued for a "rally" by a right-wing group calling itself "Patriot Prayer" at Crissy Field, a park on the city's bayfront, which NPS manages (in the end, its sponsors canceled it). The same applies to UC Berkeley's inability, or unwillingness, in the spring of 2017 to protect right-wing campus speakers, among them the inveterate self-promoting provocateur Milo Yiannopoulos, described by his campus Republican sponsors as a "contentious conservative writer, speaker," the rabble-rouser Ann Coulter, and the handful who came for a right-wing rally in the summer, from masked anarchist street mobs.

In both cases, some leading Berkeley liberals, among them Berkeley Mayor Jesse Arreguin, sounded like the southern sheriffs of the 1960s who wouldn't issue permits for civil rights marches because they couldn't protect the marchers from the local racists. To her credit, Carol Christ, who became UC Berkeley's chancellor in July 2017, made clear that the campus would be open and prepared a massive (and costly) security response for the Yiannopoulos "Free Speech Week" with its big-name speakers that, in the event, never happened.

All were ready-made events for Trumpian tweets—which probably was part of the point—and partly justification for his subsequent argument that the fatal violence attendant on the white nationalist demonstration in Charlottesville, Virginia, in August of 2017 was the responsibility of both the armed neo-Nazis and white supremacists on one side, and the peaceful counterdemonstrators who were its victims, on the other.

Most important as a possible impediment to the state's case may be the cultural gap between

California and many other parts of America—on religion, gender, gay rights, on confidence in science. Although Americans believing in a literal version of Biblical creation is reported to be down, now at 38 percent according to Gallup, the United States still ranks near the bottom among modern nations in the percentage of the population that accepts Darwinian evolution. Thus, Trump's multipronged attacks on science and scientific research were not all that surprising. Together, in the words of a *New York Times* editorial, they amount "to a war on science, appointing people with few scientific credentials to key positions, defunding programs that could lead to a cleaner and safer environment and a healthier population, and, most ominously, censoring scientific inquiry that could inform the public and government policy." That, too, is a challenge for a state so reliant on, and so committed to, science and technology—and no problem for much of Trump's base.

———————————————

IT'S HARD TO LIST all the steps of California's progress in the past two decades. The state raised its minimum wage to $15 an hour, increased the state earned income tax credit—in essence, a negative income tax for low-wage workers—and made as many as a half million more workers eligible for it. It raised its fuel efficiency standards, which were already high and have become models for thirteen other states, still higher. It's possible that Trump and Congress will try to end the waivers in the Clean Air Act that Richard Nixon signed in 1970, which allow California and the other states to set those higher standards, but it would be legally difficult. (And if they did, it's been suggested that California could do the same thing by raising the sales tax on vehicles that don't meet its standard.)

In addition, California created Secure Choice, an automatic state-sponsored retirement program for workers not covered by their employers, which is scheduled to go into effect early in 2019. Senate president pro tem Kevin de León, its sponsor, calls it the largest expansion of retirement security since 1935. It's certain to be attacked by Trump and Congress, and of course by the insurance industry—the Senate has already overturned the federal rule change that permits California to run the program. But it will be vigorously defended by the state in the courts.

Most important, the sharp expansion in MediCal, California's Medicaid program, that Obamacare made possible and that Governor Brown and the legislature implemented since 2011, drove the percentage of uninsured Californians down from 19 to 7 percent; among the beneficiaries have been thousands of undocumented minors. Fourteen million Californians now get their health care through MediCal. That number by itself is an indicator of the stakes in California's resistance. Many of the state's MediCal beneficiaries live in Central Valley districts—in Fresno County, Kern County, Tulare County—represented by Republicans. Those Republicans all voted for repeal of the ACA. Despite the Senate's failure to repeal it in 2017, they may come to regret those votes. In effect, as the battle over Obamacare makes plain, California's economic and social progress and its resistance to Trump and the Republican Congress are inseparably linked. That, too, is a portent for the future.

IN 2017, AS TRUMP WAS loading his administration with global warming deniers, withdrawing from the Paris accords, and overturning environmental regulations issued by his predecessors, including Republicans, Governor Jerry Brown was pursuing his effort to slow global warming with China and other nations—essentially advancing California's own foreign policy. (For Brown, who in his first terms as governor had wanted to create a California space program, that sort of thing wasn't altogether new.) In April 2017, Brown also hosted a meeting in San Francisco at which Canada and Mexico joined the California-sponsored Under 2 Coalition, composed of hundreds of jurisdictions—cities, states, and nations—pledged to do their share in limiting the increase in global average temperature to below two degrees Celsius. "We're looking to do everything we can to advance our program," Brown said at the meeting, "regardless of whatever happens in Washington.... We are on the side of science and truth and whatever the flimflam artists do or say, we are going to overcome that." With Trump AWOL on the issue except as a saboteur, Brown has become America's leading voice overseas on issues relating to global warming, clean energy, and the environment.

As part of that effort, Brown succeeded in getting bipartisan votes in both houses of the legislature to approve a ten-year extension (to 2030) of the state's pioneering cap-and-trade program, under which the state Air Resources Board auctions off permits to corporate enterprises allowing them to release fixed amounts of climate-changing gases, in effect pegging pollution to its economic cost. The owners can sell whatever part they don't need to others that need it more. The auctions generate hundreds of millions annually for clean air programs—subsidies for public transit, sustainable agriculture, zero-emission vehicles, and to help poor communities and individuals mitigate the effects of an unhealthful environment by, for example, underwriting air conditioning for low-income families. A chunk also goes for the tax breaks that the law's backers had to grant to get support for the extension from Republicans and business groups. (Shortly after the vote on the extension, assembly Republicans dumped Assemblyman Chad Mayes from his post as minority leader for supporting the bill and breaking with party orthodoxy. Later Mayes echoed the Schwarzenegger of a decade before: "What we've been doing for the last 20 years is not converting Californians to our ideas," he told reporter Laurel Rosenhall of CALMatters. "We've been repelling them.")

Schwarzenegger, who had signed the original cap-and-trade bill and cheered Mayes, was with Brown when he signed the extension. And as Schwarzenegger said, despite environmental programs like cap-and-trade, "we're outdoing the rest of the country in GDP." Needling Trump—whether on the sublime, like global warming, or on the ridiculous, like public approval in TV show ratings—must have given Schwarzenegger special pleasure. Like two showbiz prima donnas, the two had feuded ever since Schwarzenegger succeeded Trump as host of NBC's "Celebrity Apprentice." (For the record, Schwarzenegger didn't last long.)

THE ANTI-WASHINGTON FORCES of the Trump era in state and local government, industry and agriculture, and in countless private organizations have powerful reasons close to home for their defiance of Washington—not just moral in preventing the pain of family breakups and promising careers cut off before they could flourish, but practical in the need for labor, skilled and unskilled; in fostering enterprise and innovation; inducing cooperation with, not resistance to, police and other law enforcement agents; encouraging school attendance; averting the risk of oil spills associated with new federal oil drilling leases on the coast, as well as the environmental damage linked to further commercial exploitation of public lands; and, in the end, defending democracy. And public support for that resistance appears stronger than ever.

Jerry Brown's approval ratings as governor are nearly double Trump's as president. The approval numbers for the legislature, in 2017 at 57 percent, were at record highs. Meanwhile, as Arnold Schwarzenegger so elegantly put it, Congress was less popular than herpes.

V

HOW DID CALIFORNIA GET FROM THERE TO here? How did the state move from the anti-immigrant xenophobia of 1994 to the progressivism and the sanctuary ordinances of 2017? How did it get from the tax revolt of 1978 to three hefty tax increases some three decades later? Environmentalism had long been in the state's bloodstream, but what of the rest of it?

The most obvious element, noted above, was the rapid rise in the number of Latino voters—from 9 percent in 1992, before Proposition 187, to 23 percent in 2016. Some of them had been social conservatives on issues like abortion and gay rights, one of the things that George W. Bush and his political "boy genius" Karl Rove were counting on when they backed comprehensive immigration reform in the first years of the millennium. But beginning in 1994, many California Latinos—and many other immigrants—were driven into the Democratic camp by the Republican rigidity on immigration (and on ethnic and gender diversity generally), and most dramatically by Pete Wilson and Proposition 187—and then, of course, by Trump.

But that hardly explains all of it. The Latino share of the Texas population, at 39 percent (in 2016) is almost the same as California's, its population is 14 percent African American compared to California's 8 percent, and its state government is almost as red as California's is blue. But the Asian share of California's population (at 15 percent) is roughly three times as large as Texas' and California has a higher proportion of college graduates. And while Texas produces more wind power than any other state, its politics are still rooted in a past of gas and oil. Texas, moreover, is a southern right-to-work state, a state where employees can't be required to join a union or pay union dues as a condition of employment, and where labor has little political clout. California, in contrast, has politically powerful public sector, health care, and social service worker unions. The California Teachers Association (CTA) has long been the 800-pound gorilla of California politics, the most powerful lobby in Sacramento and a mainstay of the Democratic Party, but several others also belong on the list of heavyweights: the Service Employees International Union (SEIU), the California Nurses Association (CNA), the police and firefighters unions, the prison guards, the Operating Engineers. With the U.S. Supreme Court, now with a conservative majority, agreeing to hear an Illinois case attacking the constitutionality of contracts requiring public employees to pay agency fees to the unions that are by law required to represent them, that advantage may diminish when the case is decided in the spring of 2018. But for now, the unions are making an important difference.

Under the late Miguel Contreras, the Los Angeles County Federation of Labor brought thousands of Latino janitors, custodians, retail clerks, hospital orderlies, laborers, and other low- and median-wage immigrant workers into the movement and into active democratic citizenship. Nearly all are registered as Democrats, much in the way that the urban machines of Boston, New York, Baltimore, and other cities in the last decades of the nineteenth century once mobilized the immigrant Irish, Italians, and Poles. Perhaps not coincidentally, according to exit polls (which are always subject to uncertainty) Latinos comprised fewer than 20 percent of Texas voters in 2016, compared to the 23 percent in California. Since Trump's election, those unions have also recruited a network of private lawyers to work pro bono defending undocumented immigrants against deportation. And while public sector unions have been justly criticized for impeding reforms, as in education, or in the prison system, there has been no greater force in defense of public services and liberalism generally in the years when tax cutting seemed to be regarded as the greatest virtue in government.

But much of California's progress was also generated by the technical skills and energy—the surge of innovation and entrepreneurship—that skilled immigrants brought, and by their global connections. By the early 2000s, roughly half of Silicon Valley's executives, engineers, and computer scientists were foreign-born: Indian, Chinese, Russian, Iranian, Mexican, British. Many Asians hold dual citizenship in the United States and in their native country; many shuttle back and forth between them. Most have more in common with others of their class than they have with the nationals of one country or the other: They are, said a Stanford sociologist, himself an Indian, "a transnational elite."

And as Berkeley's AnnaLee Saxenian concluded in a major study for the Public Policy Institute of California more than a decade ago, most immigrants in Silicon Valley don't take jobs from Americans; they create jobs and foster economic development, both here and in their home countries. "Scholars and policymakers," she said, "need to recognize the growing interrelationships between immigration, trade, and economic development policy." One study in 2016 showed that half of U.S. startups worth one billion or more, a large percentage of them high-tech companies clustered in the metaphorical Silicon Valley, were launched by immigrant entrepreneurs. Silicon Valley—and much of California, indeed the whole nation—has an enormous economic stake in keeping the doors open. It's hard to imagine what "America First" means in that context.

Add to that the talent and research, despite severe budget constraints, of the state's great universities, private and public, the latter the legacy of the postwar surge of ambitious public investment in education, highways, water systems, and parks, as well as a regulatory environment that made California a national leader in reducing the emission of greenhouse gases and the use of wind and solar energy, and in more efficient use of its water resources in agriculture and other innovative technology. California uses less water now, despite its increased population, than it did twenty years ago. California's universities, said Clark Kerr, who presided over UC's great expansion in the 1960s, were "bait to be dangled in front of industry, with drawing power greater than low taxes or cheap labor." California owes Silicon Valley to Stanford and Berkeley. And then, of course, there are the beaches, the redwoods, the Sierra—the whole beauty of the state—and the climate.

IN THE 1990s, ROBERT STERN, author of the state's Fair Political Practices Act (passed in 1974 by a voter initiative) and a leading defender of the California initiative process, argued that the voters never regretted the ballot measures they enacted. But in the past decade, they and their representatives in the legislature reversed themselves, again and again, on the conservative measures they had passed a decade or two before: enacting tax increases, liberalizing the state's harsh criminal sentencing policies, granting in-state tuition status and financial aid in higher education as well as driver's licenses to the same immigrants they once excluded from both.

Two decades ago, many Republicans, among them George W. Bush, warned their fellow Republicans that exclusion of women and minorities and inflexibility on immigration, which decimated the California Republican Party after the election of 1998, could inflict similar damage on the national party. For many reasons, thanks to the Senate filibuster and relentless campaigning by opponents, the radio talkers and right-wing bloggers particularly, immigration reform didn't happen as predicted, or at least not as fast. In the election of Trump, the immigration issue had a diametrically opposite effect.

Why didn't the nation's demographic changes bite the Republicans in 2016 as Bush, Rove, and others had feared? In part, it was the partisan and racist gerrymandering and the voter suppression that the GOP engineered in a number of states in more recent years; in part, it was strategic errors by the Democrats, not least their neglect of, and sometimes their contempt for, their old blue-collar base in the Rust Belt and, ironically, their excessive reliance on the urban minorities that were (and are) a big part of the California story. In part, it was just the normal political cycle: Republican-Democrat-Republican. In part, it was FBI Director James Comey's unwarranted letter to Congress ten days before the election again raising the overblown issue of Clinton's use of her private email server for State Department business; in part, it was Russian meddling; in part, it was the intense hatred in some quarters of Clinton generated by thirty years of relentless right-wing attacks, a few of them even accurate. There was, as she said, "a vast right-wing conspiracy" against her. In part, it was the simple fact that she was a woman. And, lest we forget, she won the popular vote.

But in fact, the changing age and ethnicity of the nation's voters now seem slowly to be having their effects, despite the efforts of the GOP to stop them. In 2012, Mitt Romney beat Barack Obama in Texas by 16 points; in 2016, Trump won there by 9 points. In Arizona, which in 2010 passed its SB 1070, the most draconian of any anti-immigrant law since California's Proposition 187 in 1994, Romney won by 9 points in 2012; in 2016 Trump beat Hillary Clinton by 3 points. In 2012, the Pew Hispanic Center estimated that the 12.5 million Latinos who voted that year would double by 2030.

Maybe the most telling stories come from North Carolina, a state that narrowly went for Trump in 2016, but which elected a Democratic governor on the same day, and California itself. North Carolina, a moderate swing state, which had the fastest growing Latino population in the country in the twenty years after the 1990 census, rising from 76,000 to 890,000 in 2010, looks very much like California did a generation ago, both in its high-tech base and demographically and politically. There was an anti-immigrant backlash in 2016 as there had been in California in 1994.

But given the fact that a large percentage of North Carolina's new immigrants, many of them young, will become voters in the years ahead, the surge in Latino voting is expected to be substantial. In May 2017, the U.S. Supreme Court refused to review a lower federal court decision striking down North Carolina's voter suppression law, which had been passed by a Republican legislature and had acted, in the words of the lower court, "with almost surgical precision" to reduce the influence of African-

American voters and imposed "cures for problems that did not exist."

Contributing to the shifting results in California, Texas, and Arizona is the broader nationwide generational shift. In California as in much of the country, the young are more likely to be liberal than their elders—not just on gender and drug use, but on abortion, race, and immigration. They are more likely to have gay friends and marry, date, and have friends of other races—in brief, to be or tolerate or enjoy nearly everything that Jeff Sessions opposes. While nationwide Trump won the votes of older whites, among 20–29-year-old white women, Clinton beat Trump 51–39; among 20–29-year-old white men, she beat him 46–37.

In California, seven of the state's fourteen Republican House members, feeling increasing backlash in their districts, most of them in Southern California and in the Central Valley, over their votes to repeal the Affordable Care Act in 2017 and their support for Trump on immigration, are being targeted by the Democrats. One of the leaders in that campaign is former senator Barbara Boxer, who shortly after the 2016 election created a Super PAC that quickly raised $1.3 million for the cause. Another is former representative Ellen Tauscher of Pleasanton who formed a Fight Back California PAC that she hopes will spend $10 million by June 2018 laying the groundwork for the campaign. A third is United California, a new coalition of liberal and labor groups, partially funded by the billionaire philanthropist Tom Steyer, that's targeting the seven vulnerable Republicans. Together, those seven represent nearly a third of the twenty-four seats the Democrats need to regain control of the House.

Among them are three from districts that were carried by Hillary Clinton in 2016: Jeff Denham of Turlock, Ed Royce of Fullerton, and Darrell Issa of Vista. Issa, who, hoping to become governor himself, was a major funder of the 2003 recall campaign against Gray Davis, and once a GOP star as chair of a House committee harassing federal agencies in the Obama years, won reelection in 2016 by less than one percentage point. In May 2017, Issa and his fellow California Republicans Steve Knight of Palmdale and Tom McClintock of Elk Grove, feeling the heat, were calling for a special prosecutor to investigate the links between Trump's campaign and his associates on the one hand, and the Russians on the other. That wish was soon satisfied with the appointment of the widely respected former FBI director Robert Mueller.

Knight, Royce, and Issa, who was once tagged as a "climate change denier" by the League of Conservation Voters, joined the rapidly growing House Climate Solutions Caucus, a bipartisan group to "educate members on economically-viable options to reduce climate risk and to explore bipartisan policy options that address the impacts, causes, and challenges of our changing climate." For them and its other GOP members, the caucus may be more show than substance, but it's another small crack in their party's hard line on climate and another sign that they're feeling the heat (and the rising tides). Later, Royce would also chastise Trump for his pardon of Joe Arpaio, the thuggish former Arizona sheriff, who disregarded federal court orders to end his blatantly racist immigrant roundups.

Assuming there will be no immediate repeal of the Affordable Care Act, the biggest single headache for them all, however, was likely to be Trump's pass-the-buck decision to phase out DACA (Deferred Action for Childhood Arrivals), the program created by Obama to allow undocumented immigrants brought to this country as young children by their parents—"Dreamers"—to remain in this country, go to school, and take jobs, many of them now at the beginning of promising careers. DACA, according to *Politico*, has the support of an estimated 76 percent of the U.S. population. Trump handed off the job of preserving it to Congress, which would have six months—until March 2018—to do it. No buck stops with him.

The reaction to Trump's DACA decision was swift. Fifteen states with Democratic attorneys general and the District of Columbia, led by New York Attorney General Eric Schneiderman, immediately sued, relying in large part on the "bad hombres" attacks Trump launched against

Mexican immigrants during his campaign. "Ending DACA, whose participants are mostly of Mexican origin," the suit says, "is a culmination of President Trump's oft-stated commitments—whether personally held, stated to appease some portion of his constituency, or some combination thereof—to punish and disparage people with Mexican roots" and therefore a violation of the constitution's equal protection clause and an abuse of presidential authority. That Amazon, Microsoft, Apple, and other major corporations supported the suit was another indication of the importance, present and future, of the Dreamers in the U.S. economy.

A few days later, the University of California filed its own suit, charging that Trump's decision is "unconstitutional, unjust, and unlawful." Because of it, the complaint says, "the Dreamers face expulsion from the only country that they call home, based on nothing more than unreasoned executive whim." And because of it, "the University faces the loss of vital members of its community, students and employees. It is hard to imagine a decision less reasoned, more damaging, or undertaken with less care.... Defendants' capricious rescission of the DACA program violates both the procedural and substantive requirements of the APA (Administrative Procedure Act), as well as the Due Process Clause of the Fifth Amendment."

What made this suit, the first filed against Trump's decision by a university, particularly ironic is that as Obama's secretary of homeland security (2009–2013), UC President Janet Napolitano had both presided over hundreds of thousands of deportations—because of it, there had been vociferous student protests when she was appointed—and been Obama's author of DACA in 2012. She cited both that fact and her support for comprehensive immigration reform in her response to the student protests and promised "to be an advocate for the undocumented." It's hard to imagine that the suit wasn't one way of making good on that promise. A few days after the UC suit was announced, Becerra, citing the fact that more than a fourth of the 800,000 Dreamers covered by Obama's program are Californians, filed his own suit. "We will not permit

Donald Trump," he said in a separate statement, "to destroy the lives of young immigrants who make California and our country stronger." And no state, he said, will be more affected by the repeal than California. A few days after that, the Silicon Valley city of San Jose filed its own suit, charging that because there are Dreamers among the city's employees, meaning their loss would impair all city services, San Jose is "uniquely and directly harmed by this administration's unconstitutional actions."

Given the uncertain fate of the lawsuits, however—if Obama had the power to create the program, wouldn't Trump, despite the broken promises, have the power to undo it?—the real focus is likely to remain on Congress, and especially on members like Issa, Denham, and David Valadao, the son of Portuguese immigrants, from districts with large Latino populations. Denham, among others, was warning that "there will be a backlash against Republicans" if Congress didn't pass legislation allowing the Dreamers to stay. "We've never held kids accountable for laws that have been broken by their parents," he said in a TV interview. Trump's deal in September with the Democratic leaders of the House and Senate to support legislation restoring DACA—a deal he first denied, then acknowledged, then killed with unacceptable conditions—may give those Republicans a little cover, even as it incensed the hard-liners in Trump's party as a betrayal. What's certain, however, is that as Trump's DACA clock runs down to its March 2018 deadline, eight months before the congressional elections, the pressure on California's Republicans will continue to mount. For California's Democrats, Trump is the gift that keeps on giving.

VI

CALIFORNIA IS HARDLY WITHOUT MAJOR problems. Among them, a huge overlay of billions in underfunded public employee pension systems dating back to the tax-cutting era following the passage of Proposition 13, when revenue-constrained local governments, unable to meet employee demands for pay raises, negotiated generous pension and retiree health benefit increases that seemed cheap at the time, when health care costs were much lower and, in any case, would come due only in the distant future. The rapidly rising costs of those pensions now threaten to force cities and counties to cope with fewer teachers, cops, firefighters, and other critical workers, and cut services accordingly.

Just as worrisome: a severe housing shortage, generated in part by California's economic boom and in part by the restrictions on new housing brought by tight overlapping regulations, the state's often inflexible environmental laws, and the NIMBYism they abetted. Compounding the problem is the effect of Proposition 13's perverse property tax structure, which pegs real estate assessments to the original, relatively low purchase price, not on current value. In response, cities and counties load developers with heavy up-front fees to pay for the schools and other facilities that new residents require, adding tens of thousands of dollars to the cost of each new home.

And because the limits on property taxes made retail property that yields sales taxes more attractive to local planners than housing (and doesn't bring in more people needing more schools and other services), it was shopping malls and auto malls that got built (and are now dying in competition with online retailers). In response, home prices and rents have gone through the roof, the homeless population has mushroomed, and the state's sad, unsightly homeless encampments have proliferated along with it. In September, Brown signed a package of bills that takes some steps—but only the first—to address the housing shortage.

Nor has California's economic boom eliminated the income gap between the richest one percent, who take home roughly twenty-nine times as much each year on average, and the other 99 percent. The U.S. average is 25 to one; in New York it's 45 to one.

And while the University of California, and especially the research and graduate programs at its flagship campuses at Berkeley, Los Angeles, and San Diego continue to be regarded as models of public higher education, most of California's K–12 schools have been average at best, not just in resources but in academic achievement—and those that serve poor and minority kids often much less than average. In a state where one-fourth of students come from homes where English is not the first language and where nearly 60 percent are listed as economically disadvantaged, that's not altogether surprising, but it's nothing to brag about either. In addition, many of California's roads and freeways, once models for an auto-infatuated nation, are now a continuing embarrassment, rated among the worst in the nation. That may change as the funds being generated by the state's new infrastructure bonds become available, but it will take time. (Meanwhile, Republicans are working hard to pass a ballot measure to overturn the increased gas taxes the Democrats in Sacramento voted in 2017 to pay for them.)

And then, not to be forgotten, there are the state's deteriorating public transit systems, dams, and flood-control networks, once also models for the world. In the heavy rains in the winter of 2017, nearly 190,000 people had to be evacuated in Northern California when the spillway from the huge Oroville Dam, one of the jewels of former governor Pat Brown's State Water Project, began to fail.

More important, perhaps, while California has loosened some of the rigidity of the three-strikes sentencing law approved by the voters in 1994; passed new taxes and replaced its Depression-era provision requiring that state budgets be passed by two-thirds majorities in each house of the legislature with a simple majority requirement; and while it completely reversed itself in its treatment of undocumented immigrants, some of the major elements of the tax-cut era remain. The tight constraints on property tax assessments and local tax increases, most of which must still be passed by supermajorities of the electorate, remain in place. Proposition 13 remains sacrosanct, the classic third rail of California politics. And while the state hasn't executed a prisoner since 2006, an initiative voters narrowly passed in 2016 would speed up the state's extremely slow death penalty appeals process and make it likely that some will be executed in the years ahead.

THERE ARE COUNTLESS AREAS that are beyond the state's ability to influence, even at a time when a dysfunctional White House and Congress have been unable to pass some of the big legislation they campaigned on. There's not much California can do to stop most ICE deportations, despite the state's promise—and in some cases, the commitment by some of the state's public universities, school boards, and by Los Angeles public-sector unions—of legal aid to ICE's deportation targets, or against administration rollbacks of a long list of Obama-era regulations on everything from immigration to the ban on the sale of plastic water bottles in the national parks.

Despite some unfavorable court decisions, Scott Pruitt's EPA and Ryan Zinke's Interior Department have reversed crucial environmental regulations. In October 2017, the *New York Times* counted twenty-five rules that had been overturned and another nineteen that were on the way out. (Among them the administration's approval of the once hotly contested Keystone KL Pipeline, which was hardly noticed when it came down.) Nor can California cool Trump's gratuitous insults and his dangerous bellicosity on North Korea (condemned by, among many others, the Republican chairman of the Senate Foreign Relations Committee), or clean up the broader foreign policy mess that's eroding respect for this country and undermining relations with virtually every nation on earth. In 2017, after Trump announced yet another military lurch in Afghanistan, now the longest-running war in American history, Berkeley's Representative Barbara Lee renewed her lonely call for the repeal of the War Powers Resolution first approved, with her lone dissent, after the 9/11 attacks. She warned then that it would be "a war without end." And as San Francisco's irrepressible ex-mayor and ex-Assembly speaker Willie Brown wrote, isn't there some adult who can take the nuclear launch codes away from Trump?

In addition, and often overshadowed by Trump's daily effusions, there's the impact of the quiet undermining of federal departments and agencies, from the failure to staff key posts at the State Department to the sabotage of the EPA under Scott Pruitt who, as attorney general in Oklahoma, was closer to the polluters in the energy industry than the residents he was sworn to represent. Pruitt's blatant disregard of his own experts urging him to ban the dangerous pesticide chlorpyrifos can be mitigated in part by California's own regulatory powers. But when Pruitt packs his EPA with people like Nancy Beck, who come straight from industry groups who have long fought to undo the environmental regulations the EPA was tasked to administer; and when he greenlights the poisoning of streams and rivers in Appalachian open-pit mining; and when ICE rounds up undocumented mothers at the schoolhouse door as they drop off their children, the administration can write or rewrite policy with no new legislation and the state can do little. States can sue when Education Secretary Betsy DeVos eviscerates Obama administration rules to check fraud and exploitation of students by for-profit colleges, but even if they win, it may be hard to get her to enforce them.

Beyond that, there's the ongoing uncertainty of the impact of federal budget cuts on the billions California, like many other states, gets for everything from health care, education, and food assistance to law enforcement and road maintenance, not to mention the effects in nearly every state of Washington's ongoing administrative chaos. Other than pressing the state's own congressional delegation, or voting them out of office, there's little that Californians—not the governor, not the attorney general, not the legislature—can do there to resist Washington.

Compounding those problems is the division within the state's Democratic Party, which became bitter in the challenged election in 2017 of the state party chairman and will be exacerbated by challenges from liberals to the highly respected Senator Dianne Feinstein. That roughly mirrors the party's national split between pragmatic centrists trying (for example) to stop the slow budgetary erosion of the Affordable Care Act and Bernie Sanders' idealists calling for a politically difficult single-payer national health care system, and who complain (in an echo of the Tea Party's complaints about the GOP) that the party is too cozy with "the establishment." After Assembly Speaker Anthony Rendon blocked a bill seeking to create a state single-payer health care system that California taxpayers would never have been able, or willing, to pay for, some of his fellow

Democrats launched a short-lived campaign to have him recalled.

In those internecine battles, two important things tend to be forgotten: 1) In California, the Democrats, under their "establishment," have been winning almost everything, and 2) the Tea Party uprising on the right, which some Democratic rebels seem to regard as a model of populism, has been a disaster for the Republican agenda. Any ugly infighting within the California majority can only cloud the image of the state's economic and political success and undercut its ability to resist the pressure from Washington.

If that infighting can be resisted, and if the state can check the other pressures from the political fringes, both on the streets and in the councils of government, and if there are no unforeseen disasters—a major quake, or a national depression, or the war that Trump may have been spoiling for—all big ifs, California can make, already is making, a significant difference. At a time when states like Kansas under its tax-cutting ideologue Governor Sam Brownback are struggling with monstrous deficits and can't pay for their public schools, when New Jersey's government after eight years under Governor Chris Christie is a dysfunctional mess, and when union-busters like Governor Scott Walker of Wisconsin, using gerrymanders and voter suppression to drive the nation's red states further to the right, California, always regarded as a beacon to the American future, has an opportunity to fulfill that historic role more emphatically than ever.

California, as Harold Meyerson wrote in the *American Prospect*, "is the Trump administration's most formidable adversary not only on immigration but on damn near everything. No other entity—not the Democratic Party, not the tech industry, surely not the civil liberties lobby—has the will, the resources and the power California brings to the fight. Others have the will, certainly, but not California's clout." What America is to the world, it's sometimes been said, California is to America—and so it often has been. Even as it vigorously resists Trump, it is also the nation's preeminent un-Trump state.

"If the United States wanted to see itself as a successful world commonwealth," California's great, late historian Kevin Starr had written, "all it had to do was to look at California." And, with luck, might again. So much depends on it.

Acknowledgments

This book rests in part on work going back nearly four decades, much of it drawing on the resources and generous help of hundreds of individuals and countless organizations, public and private, too many to list here, in part on intensive research in the year after the 2016 election. But I must acknowledge the guidance of Mark DiCamillo now at the Institute of Governmental Studies, formerly at the Field Poll, and of Paul Mitchell of Political Data Inc. who helped me through the welter of conflicting 2016 election statistics.

I should also like to express my deep gratitude to two friends and ex-colleagues from the *Sacramento Bee*, Rhea Wilson and Mark Paul, who read an early draft of this essay and—all clichés aside—made valuable suggestions. And as always, thanks to my most trusted and patient reader, Patricia Ternahan, for whom I'm grateful for ever so many things.

I've long admired Heyday for its warm and wise devotion to California places, nature, and history, but until recently I never thought anything I might write would fit into Heyday's list. Now Donald Trump has brought us together, which is probably the only thing I'll ever thank him for. And so my gratitude to my editor Steve Wasserman, Heyday's publisher, who I admired when he was the editor of the *Los Angeles Times Book Review* and, from my experience, is as sharp making books as he was reviewing them.

About the Author

PETER SCHRAG served for nineteen years as editorial page editor of the *Sacramento Bee* and has long followed California affairs. A former executive editor of *Saturday Review,* he is the author of articles and reviews in the *Atlantic, Harper's,* the *Nation,* the *New Republic,* the *New York Times,* the *Los Angeles Times,* and the *Washington Post,* among other publications. His *Paradise Lost: California's Experience, America's Future* was a *New York Times* Notable Book in 1998. Among his recent books are *Not Fit for Our Society: Immigration and Nativism in America* (2010) and, with Otto Schrag, *When Europe Was a Prison Camp: Father and Son Memoirs* (2015). A former Guggenheim Fellow, and for many years a visiting scholar at the Institute of Governmental Studies at the University of California at Berkeley, he has taught at Amherst College, the University of Massachusetts, and at UC Berkeley's Graduate School of Journalism and its Graduate School of Public Policy. He lives in Oakland.

About the Publisher

HEYDAY is an independent, nonprofit publisher founded in 1974 in Berkeley, California. It promotes civic engagement and social justice, celebrates California's natural beauty, and promotes Indian cultural renewal. Through books, public events, and outreach programs, Heyday works to give voice to the voiceless and to realize the California dream of diversity and enfranchisement. For more than thirty years, it has published *News from Native California*, the state's leading magazine of Indian affairs. Heyday seeks to build a vibrant community of writers and readers, activists and thinkers.

DISCARD

A Note on Type

TRUMP MEDIAEVAL is named after Georg Trump, its designer, who created it between 1954 and 1962. An old-style serif typeface, it was used both by the C. E. Weber foundry as metal type and Linotype for hot metal typesetting. Its classical aspect recalls earlier Venetian typefaces and is commonly associated with books of enduring merit and bespoke design. Pleasing to the eye, it is a font of balance and serenity whose proportions and aesthetic appeal are widely admired by typographic connoisseurs the world over.